RUSH TO THE LAKE

RUSH TO THE LAKE

poems by

FORREST GANDER

ALICE JAMES BOOKS
Farmington, Maine

ACKNOWLEDGMENTS

The author wishes to thank the editors of the following
publications in which poems, sometimes in different form,
first appeared: *Caliban, The Chariton Review, Cutbank, Five
Fingers Review, Gargoyle, Hollins Critic, Northeast Journal,
Phoebe, Poetry Now, Quarry West, The Quarterly, Raccoon,
Stone Country, Swallow's Tale, Transfer, Tyuonyi, The William
and Mary Review.*

Alice James Books are published by the Alice James Poetry
Cooperative, Inc., an affiliate of the University of Maine at
Farmington.

Alice James Books
238 Main Street
Farmington, ME 04938
www.alicejamesbooks.org

Library of Congress Cataloging-in-Publication Data
Gander, Forrest
Rush to the lake
I. Title
PS 3557.A47R87   1988   811'.54   87-72606
ISBN 0-914086-78-2 (cloth)
ISBN 0-914086-79-0 (pbk.)
ISBN-13 978-0-914-08679-6 (pbk.)

The publication of this book was made possible with support
from the Massachusetts Council on the Arts and
Humanities, a state Agency whose funds are recommended
by the Governor and appropriated by the State Legislature.
Alice James Books gratefully acknowledges support from the
University of Maine at Farmington and the National
Endowment for the Arts. ❦

The reprinting of this book was supported by a grant from
the Frank M. Barnard Foundation.

*Typeset by the Writer's Center
Designed by Forrest Gander
Cover Art: Il Tuffatore (fresco, 470 B.C., Italy)*

for the poet C.D. Wright

and for Lida Junghans, Mike Perrow, Mark Craver,
Tom Duffy, Henri Cole

contents

I

SYMPATHY FOR THE NOVITIATE

. . . as the retainer Benkei, and Yoshitsune escape
across the tiger's tail called Minato River

Shizuka labors on a splintered floor
and kneads Yoshitsune's son, feet first, out of her.
Her small teeth are set deep
into a wedge of green bamboo.
Soldiers searching for the ex-lieutenant
find her shaved
and dressed as a boy.
They catch her through the window
nursing an infant
whose head they will place on a rock
in the newly raked garden.

At this moment the famous pair
are slipping past a border blockade
disguised as monks.
Purposely they stutter vows
like nervous birds
since imitation, if pressed too far,
will cease to impress a likeness.
In this way they fly another night
through an absent-minded terrain, the smell of apples
while Shizuka hangs by her ankles
and is branded by village policemen.

Finally the heroes are ambushed,
their hired men drop their burdens
of loyalty. Benkei bends, brushing fingertips
in sand by the water. He staves off
thirty men, the long rib of his sword,
his kimono going black,
the silence of frogs.
Frozen in a defensive position
called "total awareness
in pretense of distraction,"
                              he leans
on the hilt, grinning.
The men are afraid to attack him.
They find no vulnerable point.

In the palanquin just behind, Yoshitsune
titles his legendary death poem.
Shizuka is cut down and carried
to a convent,
unrecognizable, not yet twenty.
The wind blows Benkei over. He has been dead.

Before they reach him
Yoshitsune, the ex-lieutenant,
gently poises his dagger
ornamented with gold phoenixes
and thinks of summer evenings by the river,
boat lights.

And Shizuka goes on living
the long steady pain his legend admits no part of.

II

Island of broken horses

THE PLOT

Where a man loves a woman there is an island
of broken horses, stranded wheelbarrows
listing with cement. Morning is a flat blaze.
She boils water. Nervous hands.
Early, the husband steps out
on the false porch. Clouds rise.
The nail of sun, it will hold.
She goes in and out shaking
damp rags. He hears her in the cabinets.
On the warm splintering steps
the man hunkers: their breach, this field.
Two Clydesdales are fucking
like the carcass of one Oldsmobile
piled on another. Next to the fence
a rock works its way out of dirt.
The black bar in the gold circle
of the goat's eye
shifts. The path stinks, musty as a snake.
Markings red and brown, and of good size.

THE DIAGRAM

In this corner my desk

Here
Behind a panel under stairs
We roll the bedding to sleep

In the center of our long room
I unfold a futon
Over the heater

Winter nights

We sit with the children
Wrapped in a cold lava
Colored quilt
Watching tv

Which recently I have removed
        there
It is not a crowded neighborhood
Voices carry warari-warari

My garden's hypotenuse
Rushes into borrowed scenery
A view from each window
Of the February moon

In this room is my study
In this room my husband's mirror

KATA: BUS STOP

I love this
hill here   light   the mountain

    hidden like Fuji
in Hokusai's sketches by a tidal wave
of fog

    which collapses
over habits of
waking up   coffee   standing for the bus
that re-enact themselves

    on every block,

re-enact

    : that bus for the standing,
    coffee,
    waking themselves up to

habits which collapse
                on every block
like a tidal wave
of Hokusai's sketches

Hidden in fog,
          the mountain
      light here
            this hill I love

DISTRACTIONS FROM THE REAL WORLD

Someone has been undressing
in my room. She works
over my body at night
with long-nailed fingers.

I wake with breath on my lips,
a sweating hide. Things irrevocable,

for me the several shits of the troubled.

Next door my neighbor is also
showering, cold water
in the semi-light.

Last week he told me he kicked a can
from 3rd St. to 22nd
before he felt stupid.
By the time he fell in bed though
he was obsessing
about the can. He yanked his pants on
and a ski jacket, went out
to find and kick the can
the hell home. He walked
about an hour, stopped
at a donut place and bought a regular coffee.

On weekends I work for a quadriplegic
whose wife is beautiful.
When I sleep in the next room
they make love, quiet as heat lightning.

The 3 of us visited 2 men
who own a vineyard. They brought out
bottles without labels like the natives

of this valley who never carved faces on their dolls.
The man I work for knows
about wine. I brought the glass
to his lips.
There were empty bottles.
It was midafternoon.

The woman stood up stretching,

sweat transparentized parts of her blouse.
She said Is that a pool? The owner
answered Yes. She asked Is it
alright to take a swim,
(he said I'll get you a towel)
I didn't bring a suit.
Her husband looked from his wheelchair.
The man came with a white towel.
She lifted the latch and closed the gate
behind. Everyone sat back down.
After a minute we heard her body
enter the water. Her husband
mentioned fumé blanc, the owner told why
he doesn't grow that grape.
We reached for our glasses

waylaid by the dark hair,
the arc of her kicking
feet behind the thin wood slats.

That night I rubbed her back
in the living room across from her husband,
his chair. Dreaming like he was.
My hands, his.

I watched the late show, *An Officer And A Gentleman,*
which is a movie about factory workers
not having a dream
except to put out when they are shat on
until a man dressed in white
carries one of them
away. Then everyone claps they are so happy.

Earlier in the day
crack men in Florida
taught soldiers flown from Honduras
tricks Americans know,
how to cripple what they touch.
Kurosawa tells it:
                    the bad sleep well.

THE LAST CASTRATO

The first time Yuko used the vibrator
after I tried to get her to come for so long
she kept climaxing one after another
more beautiful than a strange language.

I watched in the dark like Li Po
whose optimism was philosophical
obligation
in a poem without figures.
The dull loneliness over the greener veins,

sometimes I drop to bed out of fear.
Rub my feet for their familiar smell.
I limp over the undiminished mesa
of desire, singing,

my fingers curled into my hands.
This soft dry heaving in my wrist
like a slim-waisted woman who sleeps.
Things I cannot say.

PARABLE OF THE TINDERBOX

: how, looking for the tinderbox, a witch
comes down the road one night,
the witch being a white deer, a deer
with a woman leading him.
On the road she meets a soldier. He has
lips dangling to his waist. Keep in mind
it is the deer who is the moon and not the woman.
The soldier climbs the hollow tree.
He says Beg pardon, ma'am, but that's my deer.
He is pointing to the moon.
The woman's hair is parted in the middle, her
labia show. She discovers she likes to eat briars.
The soldier enters the hollow tree, finds
a wide tunnel lit by lamps. He sees three doors
with keys in their locks. In the first room
opposite a spinning wheel,
against the wall,
sits a chest
                    with a living hound on top,
its eyes like muddy wheel wells.
He uses the witch's apron. She has limped to the cabin.
He picks up the dog, sets it on the apron, fills his knapsack
with copper. The witch is stretched on the floor.
                                           Cold
                   wind catches in the hollow tree.
There is a sound like a shakuhachi, peacocks fucking.
The dog in the next room has eyes big as ferris wheels.
It straddles a chest of silver.
When the soldier lays down the witch's apron
a splinter catches the hem, eleven
princes are turned to swans.

He dumps the copper
from his knapsack. What is the dog staring at?
And scatters the silver as he bolts
for the next room,
turns the key, kicks the door.
There is nothing. Less. Nothingness.
He wheels around but the moon
is a naked eye
swinging toward him.
He tips into black
     kissing the apron
for luck. By the hollow tree
a deer carcass is plucked by seven crows.
She was a child full of smiles.
The season shifts, the frozen rain
crystallizing dew on clumps of grass
which glisten like mons venus.
No one returns from this story
although you may look up and clearly see the last moon,
the first soldier, the white deer with
a woman naked and sexless riding toward us
from a country where Lapt Blumen sprechen.
But she always dies
of her deer, because in this country
the cure ensures its disease.

RUINED TUNNEL

One of them   drops radio into hardhat
        and spits, Damn it,
        boys, we won't need this one.
But hell, they had already drilled
the charge. In the dynamite's
wake, boulders turn to snow.
Men walk through the trees.
        It's cool now in here.
Quiet enough
to hear tracks rust;
the Monte Ne line that never whistled through
and the summering passengers
unstartled by sudden dark,
the temperature drop.
Stones jut out,
gargoyles scabbed with lichen.
The steamy eye
of an afternoon
watches us from either end.
        We are waylaid by a spell.
A stone
slithers off
or I imagine this.
In the pitch I feel
the others when they breathe.
We are unborn. One
of our silhouettes speaks,
        There's a camera in the car.
Bats opening like orchids.
The absence of one of us, unimaginable—
our present so intense
its tense is aorist.
Each of us afraid to leave
two men he loves behind.

IMAGINING YOU

It would be good to see them again
The pink roofs of their mouths
Startled by cold, their long sighs
Mushrooming into air

It would be like a break
In the weather
Their sounds among the sounds
That kick up frost
Scatter aphids in the roses
When all the exhausted
Can do is sleep

Veering balletically around corners
To arrive at a door
Their breath held
Like a pair of shoes
Outside the rooms
Where sisters of our friends
Have turned beautiful

They sit lightly on an edge of bed
Staring into your face
As though it were night
Their blind hands
Under the blankets, over
Your woman's breasts
Without thinking, out of memory

Tipped back in the broken chair
They hesitate to finish the bottle
All they have seen is misfortune
Lodging in the lovelier bodies

The willow who was a friend
Has gone, the one thing
That has changed

RUSH TO THE LAKE

Who is allowed in the inner
circle by the boathouse
to see the drowned schoolgirl?
The father crouched like a black rock.
The lover, his lower lip shivers.
A little back, the mother
stands, blinking.

The impassive water
has slipped her
its cold tongue.
The nuns hold back the children
who are straining to the edge
of their faith
for the dead to be like the wonderful
dead in stories.

THIN LIPS

The executioner's delicate son doesn't walk
to school after a black Sunday.
But the other boys
miss the late bell on Tuesday too.
They clamor into desks
they've outgrown, flushed
and out of excuses
betting he won't come one day this week.
The child lays back
in the scratchy loft.
He stares as a milk snake
slips into the unlimed straw
warm with manure.
While the other boys are having wet dreams
he listens to rain
drumming metal. Closes his eyes
against his father's whisper,
You are my only son.

THE NEAR SUICIDE OF LEON RAPOLLO

The floor of Lake Pontchartrain is littered with clarinets.
Anyone can see them
who is drunk, in the shallows at night,
unburrowing in pieces
like species of trilobite. Stick your head in,
wade out. They are attracted
when you blow out your breath.

THE MOMENT WHEN YOUR NAME
IS PRONOUNCED

This high up, the face
eroding; the red cedar slopes
over. An accident chooses a stranger.
Each rain unplugs roots
which thin out like a hand.
Above the river, heat
lightning flicks silently
and the sound holds, coiled in air.
Some nights you are here
dangling a Valpolicella bottle,
staring down at the flat water
that slides by with its mouth full of starlight.
It is always quiet
when we finish the wine.
While you were a living man
how many pictures were done
of you. Serious as an angel,
lacing up your boots. Ice
blows into my fields.

AN EROTICS FOR AGONY

Stood waiting for the 990
                              lb. animal
                to fall
        But suddenly
turned suddenly, suddenly
                              the bull
                turned
                              Stood waiting
Yijo, meaning "little
                              boy" the last
                minute
                gored
as the sun was setting
                as he delivered the estocada
                              his final sword
                                              thrust
                              as the sun
                stood, waiting
                              for Burlero, a name
that means joker
                        to fall
        This bull has killed me
                              his assistant said
                        were his final words
                catching him in the heart
                                              tip
of its left horn
                              standing him
                straight up in the air

LOT'S WAGES

The Hunter rises on his back in the Blue Ridge.

To the man nicking his face
in the mirror it is the anniversary
of another man's death.
There is a woman on the couch,
his coffee cup on the sink,
agony of flies.

Clean shaven, the man stands
shaking his dick. He walks
lightly through the dark rooms
as by prescience, starts the car.

What could he give her?

In the rearview mirror
her eyes are soft as goodnights
spoken to hair.

Valences of insects
brushing the porchlight.
She leans against the door,
notices dampness
at the base of her spine.
She knows her love
to be a cenotaph.

Reaching back as he drives
he scratches a scar on his shoulder blade
until it bleeds,
feels nothing but pressure.

CAT, CLARINET, AND TWO WOMEN

I mail letters
not knowing your address.
Rooms of dust

are written to you, directly.
Though you have come to be all but
　　imaginary.
Each day I spend in the world

the stupid dog bawls.
But what is happening to your voice.

As your real voice goes deeper
sleep grows in my ears
over your old words
which are like moths in daylight.

You are broken into two
voices, a parallel evolution.
Parallel, but not equal.

Yet how can I complain
when women with your famous eyebrows
are lifting their red skirts
and dancing with castanets
all night on the roof of my pain.
I could not complain
unless they are a downpour.

I think of everything
that is given back
in being given.
Backrubs, orgasm,
a death poem.

AFTER HAGIWARA

A child was pulled from the lake.
The schoolmates whispered into each other's ear.
They whispered a dirty story
into each other's funny, shell-shaped ear.
The wind backed off.
On the bed lies a woman.
In her face,
two eyes.

CITRUS FREEZE

To the north, along Orange Blossom Trail,
thick breath of sludge fires.
Smoke rises all night, a spilled genie
who loves the freezing trees
but cannot save them.
Snow fine as blown spiders.
The news: nothing.
Large rats breed on the beach
driving smaller ones here.
Today both traps sit sprung.

NEW PROOF DEATH COMES AFTER LIFE

Each evening the dog pisses
on the same stone, Parolini.
The three caretakers in their home
may be brothers and sister,
not talking or watching tv.
The woman looks at her hands,
one man stares. I can't tell about the other.
They are as visible through the picture
window of their living room
as a slide under a microscope.
For the dull class of headstones
with such slow vision, they must appear
to scurry around the lighted room
like parameciums, and then I zoom up; odd,
this close in the dark
knowing they can't see me.
When the dog humps over, his tail
is the handle to a pump
a ghost is working for water
or I imagine this, imagine
asking for water, being served shit.

THE DRESS REHEARSAL MYTH

Angelica's orange hair whipped her face
when she woke chained to the chasm
and the sea serpent
rolled under waves
like a lathe spinning in an oil bath.
All the Valkyries were just foam
shot through the air in long swatches.
I was in the stables
hanging the bevelled mirror,
dusted with lime.
Angelica threw her face forward
and her hair burned
her breasts, the cerulean gown
had slipped and bunched
below the delicate down
at the base of her back.
She was sick of waiting for me
to brush my hair and mount my horse.
Slowly the dark came
like Helen Traubel's voice.
Callouses on Angelica's hands
like lie over lie over lie.
I pulled on my white trousers
and winched the saddle tight.

III

Sumō

Ø   Ø   Ø

As it would for a desk, the crowd
parts around him, though he is moving
also, as fluidly as lips are read;
something poured from hand to hand.

Crowds excite him. It is what
he sees of the others. Living apart, eating
apart. Training. On the streets
he is everyone's borrowed scenery.
His is a quiet
no music enters. But the twilight
rush hour does not
feel rude. As he walks

he separates the noise into chromatics,
constant pitch becoming pulses.
His steps function to maintain
the ground rhythm by which everything else
is syncopated.

∅   ∅   ∅

It is the semi-light of morning.
Picture a man weighing 370 pounds
standing before a dark mirror
alone, in a small room, naked,
mesmerically braiding his long hair.

∅   ∅   ∅

His clumsiness looks like cruelty as he pays for dinner,
the greater part of which was saké,
and aims himself like a bowling ball
at the elegant cluster near the door
waiting to be seated.

He holds a loxodromic course for the docks,
wonders how many people have noticed
the parted limbs in this tree.
Attempting to return to the path
I came to the fork
and went both ways it hasn't
made any difference.
His tongue works the itch
back of his throat.
If his mouth wasn't prickling
dry, he would want a lover,
and to run his tongue along that ligament
thin as an expensive pen
which touches torso to paperwhite thigh.
Walking the pier it is his body
thinking. *All the fishing boats*
are named for the same woman.
She runs the only dock restaurant
anybody goes to.
No one set her up, I've heard
those lies. All night gulls
are circling her house. Plenty
of married men spill their love there.

Stepping over a sewer cap it occurs to him
he would like to own a kimono just that color
so he could walk invisibly
through the rain that has started.

∅   ∅   ∅

Throughout this scene he doesn't move.
At each of several stops, others jerk
for the door haltingly— the way
spiders crawl. Or spill out of the train,
new bodies cramming in so that
the density remains about the same.

In motion again, they fumble with coats
to let heat out
like water from a shell.
A woman's hood falls back
and she shakes steam loose from her hair.
He is staring.
She is the color of wet shale and koto music
in the morning. She is gone
at the next stop, and then he sees
through the window, an instant before the crowd
settles in, her double face
refracting through the glass, her lips,
brake lights in rain.

∅ ∅ ∅

Suits mostly, suits
Western suits
grey as the caps in his teeth.

There is a shorter man
staring into the wrestler
like a blind animal by a wall.
At the lower edge of his vision,
headlines under the man's arm:
Nakasone suggests merger,
a woman shuffles between.
His gaze floats back over the tops of heads,
Western hats, a white scarf
with iridescent dots like beetles.

∅　　∅　　∅

He sees himself with Nakasone
under lights, the same density in the air
of a crowd. He is hauling Nakasone up
by his mawashi, leaning over the flailing
body, forcing it backwards;
he shoves his own face
close and smells tobacco.
With their eyes inches apart
he bites off the tip of Nakasone's nose
and chews it.

Opposite, where the white wall
curves into ceiling
are advertisements.
Lawyers offer service. Photo
of pottery above the characters
*Sacred Art of Onisaburo Deguchi and the
Oomoto Community.*
A green poster reads: *Mamushizake,
saké in which a poisonous viper is steeped.*
His testicles rise.

Ø   Ø   Ø
the room

To inanimate objects even our slightest moves
are amazing. Walls do not blink.
His footsteps handsome
in the silence, his shuffle
to unroll the futon.
He lays down— a verb surrounded by nouns,
the message in a bottle. Sleep
demands its rituals. There is the familiar return
of images, like water over terrain.
He licks his palm and anoints the head
under the quilt. He strokes himself
to his imagination and the barking
of his heart. The floor recalls
muffled nuzzling. The walls— color
blaring across the room. An intensity
abrupts: white caps, horses,
breasts float up like beautiful jellyfish,
a human gift is burning like a flower.

∅ ∅ ∅
image

first step: kill turtle

punching is not allowed
use a thrusting slap
to the chest-throat region

into a boiling pot of seaweed
dump turtle chicken
pork sprouts angel
hair onions

stand with feet
apart, suck in breath
tip the body left
raising right leg
sideways high as possible then:
stamp down
with a hissing exhale
five hundred times

in the open adjacent room
taking the visitor's request
for sushi,
the addlepated novice
whose face gleams like cold tea

lean forward, legs
spread 180 degrees
pressing upper body
navel to cheek-
bone against floor
the senior wrestler may help
by standing on your back

bowl
upon bowl
wash down
     with
          quarts of beer

the winner declared
by a 14th century noble, brandishing
a warrior's fan

elapsed: 7.5 seconds
time it takes
to let the other mass
          fall

Ø Ø Ø
anti-image

first step: bowl
       upon
       navel

with a hissing exhale
the senior wrestler thrusts
into the novice
spread 180 degrees, bone
against floor

the onion-face visitor may help
pressing upper body, part
feet, placing cheek against tip
of turtle

stand with cold tea
raising hair gleams
to the chest-throat region

in the adjacent room
7.5 quarts of beer elapsed
high as possible
five hundred requests for sushi

the winner punching a 14th century noble
into a boiling pot of seaweed
tip the body left
then stamp down

take its time
let the angel
           fall
by standing on your back

Ø   Ø   Ø

No matter how good you are, something
happens and you live in the shadow
of that event. I pushed the elevator
button. I was thirteen, lonesome,
visiting. My friends napped.
I stood front of the doors as it came falling

down the shaft, falling
while I thought of something
I'd forgotten: to wash my face. The cord snapped
in silence in the shadow
of the penthouse floor where some lonesome
man had stepped out. The elevator

doors closed behind him and elevator
detached itself, cable falling
away like dock rope; not lonesome
but mediocre as any fact. If something
in the universe altered in the shadow
of the lobby, I was worrying with the snapped

shirt button between my fingers. No signal snapped
me out of myself. The elevator
was a pear in the ripening shadow
of the hoist. Its falling
speed increased like a sum. Things
I had no control over left me lonesome

in those days. There was beauty and lonesome
humiliation; I was not faithful to either. A woman snapped
her fingers and took the stairs. Something
made me want to race. I touched the elevator
button and it began its falling,
clipping the walls and the metallic shadow

of each floor as water surges in a ravine past shadows
of trees. I was adrift outside the lonesome
couple which links life and death by their falling
against each other. My fists snapped
shut and fell open like cracked nuts. The elevator
cage hit bottom and something

snapped my jaw and broke it cleanly in the shadow
of the elevator doors. They were rent open, the lonesome
cage burst out and something changed in me as I was falling.

Ø   Ø   Ø

The wrestler, dressed in his best formal
kimono, his oiled hair combed
into the handsome oichomage knot,
sits in the middle of the dohyo.
Beside him stands a high referee
in ceremonial tournament dress
holding a pair of gold plated scissors.
One by one friends,
relatives, fellow wrestlers
climb into the ring
to take a ritual snap at the back
of the knot. When the yokozuna Wajiima
retired in November 1981, it took 320 men
an hour and a half to cut his hair
all the while he was weeping.

∅   ∅   ∅

One evening in summer I follow him from a restaurant to his dohyo. The way his feet fall, his body doesn't actually sway. Only the slightest list from side to side. His kimono (something else that marks him since most Japanese in Tokyo dress "Western style") is dark and light blue, plain except for a white bird between his round shoulders, with a pink flower in its beak. It is the representation of *yugen*, "what lies beneath the surface."

I imagine his shoulder blades sinking in and back with the light swing of his arms. I think he must be sweating, even though it is cool, just from inertia. But I am wrong. The fabric is light, sweat would show through. Occasionally his fingers stretch out from each other and he rotates them. Just as I am noting this he has bent and plucked something up which scuttled across his sandal like a plover from a wave. Without breaking stride, his stooping no more than a nod. It is trash, a tissue spilled from someone's purse or coat pocket, anyone's in the crowd. I glimpse it just once, enough to see two crescents of red lipstick, before he tucks it into his cavernous sleeve.

Oh, one other thing I remember. There is a dirt path to the dohyo where his sandals leave ripple marks. After he had entered, I tried to retrace his steps, careful to place my right foot exactly where he had placed his right foot. I had to stretch my legs as though running away from an ogre.

Ø   Ø   Ø
the mother

I was so pregnant
I thought I could break open
with the touch of a fingernail
like a rain-soaked cigarette.
When my son was born
his twin was born
dead. Doctors told me
put a clock in the cradle,
he'll sleep. His name
means Smoke in the Roots
of my Hair. We settled
near apple country and I watched him
waste a childhood
singing to crows.

By the time he was twelve he was
terrifying. He was already
gone, like a burglar,
like a picking season, an orgasm.
He was gone like the glasses
of the first girl who touches him.
Like the names of neighbors,
odor of aftershave.
Like a stray pet, the way
he cried into its fur
through bad nights.
Like the dew sweeper the swordbearer.
He left like 47 ronin to avenge a death
except he left to avenge
his illegitimate birth. He left like
heat from a room.
He was gone, a voice
on the telephone as snow
falls through the line.

IV

Pitched against small fires

SCAFFOLDING AND WIND

The child showed what she
learned in school today.
Guess what this is she said
cracking both hands together
over her father's head
and running her fingers lightly
down the sides of his face.
"An egg?" he said.
No, your heart.

CONVERSION TO A DAMNED NIETZSCHE

I am the serpent at the end of decadence.
An ocean imitates the fall
and rise in my veins.
She said, One response to
beauty is transformation.
I disembark from journeys
into well-lit eyes.
My balls are two lumps of charcoal.
Although you bathe, she said, in warm
rooms of conversation, you
will die unbaptized, childless, and full of pain.
She said, You are what is wrong
with this picture, have a good time
if we don't see you.
I am so gentle it begins to rain.
Open the curtains, she explained,
you will see a mirror.
I shot the deputy.
I wonder how things would be
had I stayed.
Inscribed on my tombstone:
Drink constantly,
Fuck everyone
But do not sleep
Do not marry
And do not work
For an asshole.
The petite, she said, authority of ignorance.
My garden is grief.
Because there is not much time

I say only marvellous things.
First, was it you,
she asked, on the earth breathing
without us, and then
how was it different?
I woof in my sleep
and sleep under the empty quarter
drifting deathward. My left eye
is Beid the egg, my right eye
Reid the shell.
She said, You would rename yourself the.
I am tipped off
to men of little faith,
there is a bug in my ear.
She said, We cannot remember what you are like.
Inside me a wolf shivers its mane.

LOITER

I'll know the time to leave the room
where I've been growing hair
from my face, drinking dark beers
when the light in the lake burns out.
That's when fish
turn on their music.
They lie in a blue current
waiting for the moon
to pass over, and the fishermen
with their lanterns know this
as they spill a can of sweet corn
and wonder if they spoke
what they were just thinking.

I clear my way through the fog
as music will break through static.
The frogs strike up,
a window goes out
in the Home for Elders.
Don't you wonder why
it is built far from anywhere,
as though memory needs a terrain
for forgetting; blind
driveways to lost roads.
As for my own parents, they did not
grow old. What I know:
dinners without conversation,
stars that shine for anyone.
I know my time
is brief. I know love of the cut sleeve.

I want to say
don't feel sorry for men,
those who leave women
smouldering like cigarettes,
those who are fond of burials.
War is a habit of mind,
I swear by my mother's gender.

Tonight sticks in the leaves
are slick as pilot snakes.
Wherever I part branches
no one is in a boat,
no one has stirred a wake.
Not jackknifing off the dock,
it's hauling myself back up
that gooses my titties and makes my peter shrink.

Don't wake the cottonmouths.
Summertime. If you were here
and you remembered to stash your smokes
in a Glad bag so they didn't soak like mine
we'd fall quiet now as pollen
on water, I would
tell you the true story of Urashima
and the turtle.

THE FACE OF ANOTHER

Pitched around small fires
run through with wind,
soldiers snore.
Torches splash their tents
with simulacra of rifles
tethered to bamboo,
stiff men dropping dice.
Some spit in their sleep.
Along the shallow moat
the lifeless shift like swollen fish.
A letter home: the moon whole.
Cross-legged, massive right forearm
planted on a stool, Tokugawa
pulls his mustache absently
like a woman opening
and closing an exquisite fan.
He aches to hear the enemy flute,
his soldierly eyelids crust
with snow. The staffs that mark his chair
rattle in the dirt. When the flutist
mounts the wall, those awake halt
their conversation to listen.
Others waken.
Wind whipping torches,
snapped cloth.
Inside the fortress, men
hear the same music
in sleep, grappling their wives.

WOMAN IN THE DUNES

Sand in the morning blurs her nipples,
the sun in storm. Light,
liquid sand, capillary flow.

Not-having drives the man. Insect collector is
insect. Quick sand, slow water.

The woman, exhausted, gets up from bed to sponge the thick-
thighed man.

Wind ripples, hieroglyphs under tide pools.
The mass of it snaking. One grain between teeth.

Rope ladder drops from above the pit. Villagers are perching.
Intransible phalanx cut loose. Tatami. Umbrella covers
steamed rice. The dog-breath foehn, hiss.
Tinkling. Crow trap bucket. Bread crumbs, blackness
from the cave as bats, hive of bees explodes. A star
falling off a constellation.

The corner of her eye takes root. She moves like water spilling.

Villagers buoyed around the edge. Their voices so much
like wind, she always hears them. She doesn't love anything
more than this.

They quarrel like tired blades: ritual, a cul-
tivation of beauty.

The woman spits a tooth. Her kimono darkens from the armpits
in the morning. All night sand filters back, falls through
cracks in bamboo. The moon catches sand drifting into the
house like music; the woman, her lost details.

Before he comes, when she wakes she prays
a strong man falls into the pit.

ONO NO KOMACHI

The cut bamboo fence; wind
cruises the hollow posts.
Near the window, Ono No Komachi burns
candles. The lover would walk
his long way, pausing
at the gate. Each night in October
he did not pass the gate. Not in November,
not ever. Her kimono —
color of scraped rust —
glows through the slatted window, all warmth
escaping his body, her hair
black as wicks. She watches him
shape his doughy breath
to his hands and spit
red at the snow.
When he takes the blade
from his sleeve she notices again
his eyes in the dark
like an animal's. He stabs below
the last notch, the green bamboo
blazed with his notches, and he
turns, propped against invisible
wind; withdraws like a recurring
character in a child's dream
with his face hooked by the lighted room.
When his ghost came
to carve the hundredth notch
it trudged through the gate, curled up
like smoke in Ono No Komachi's eyes.
Her reflection frosting at the mirror,
she blows out, she turns old.

EVENING CALM

After the strangling of each first son
an overture of sighs
floated the streets.
You think of this
watching fog.
It lifts off the lake
like a soldier getting up
from a foreign war. He halts
on your land for a drink. Water
clouds over and churns in your well.

Outside hundreds stumble by.
They are not injured. You,
not dreaming. Another drifts
down your path who does not want water.

The moon depends from the earth
like an ear. While the cold

ferrets into your lungs,
boots crack the garden's hard pan.
These are the ones past thirst
trained by strangers with latches

softly clicking in their voices.
In the pitch they see
every detail. They've come

to return something. Not their gear.
Their hands clench and open like flowers.
When you approach the garden
ruby-throated birds fly.

RAFT OF THE MEDUSA

I was crying in the stall while he waited to piss

You turned from the bar with a Salem 100
In your mouth and one smoking
At your fingers
Not expecting me
You look bad you said
Where you been
So long
I said I hauled some roosters
To Delaware I got loaded
Thinking I'd never see the ocean
And I drove the truck
So deep in sand
I had to climb out my window
And every one drowned
By morning

He found me she said
And he stalks over
Saying This loser
I crack my fingers
Duke here play trombone for you
Or something
I said
I played a stack of dimes
Into the phone from Delaware honey
But you were never home
She started crying and the band
Laid in, I don't know why
They learn all the riffs
And don't give a shit about sound

I woke up out of town
In a vineyard with everything tortured
And crucified in rows
I lost my amulet too
But it never worked
Nothing could stop me
Remembering the view
Coming up over the hills
Of your breasts

PSYCHOANALYSIS OF MUSIC

No lie, those who strolled to the end
Of the block are gone

It doesn't happen winter evenings
But it does in the evening
When air cools
And takes your washed hair
In its fingers

There is a chill like a lover
Touching you here
And here, who strokes your throat
like a kite's

Through kitchen windows,
An opened door,
The ones who see you
Are reminded of statues, stares
Locked on the infinite
Regresses

Your footsteps are soft as plums
In the ripening darkness

In an envelope you don't carry
The words flood
Flood

Ahead, shoes hang from telephone wire
Three stars cut Orion
Night's clouds parting like thighs
All clear as a name
Chiselled in marble

The bars over the last windows
You walk past are thickening
Strings stripped from the fingers
Of Mingus

It is done in one take

THE DROWNING OF YUKO

When Brady stepped off the dune he had on
a raincoat twisting behind him.
The rest of us stood up together
like hair on a dog's shoulder.
Yuko said the raincoat moved him

the way a Bunraku doll is moved from behind
by a figure in black.
I had to sit down
to pull off my pants
while the others were reading sand.

She was desperate to talk.
I threw palmfuls of water
in my eyes.

Yuko was wading naked through the white shadow
thrown by the sun.
Her nipples dark as vinegar, her hair
floated. I said don't
look directly at the sun.

Just her head showed now.
We were all on the beach holding
our breath. The sun ducked under,
hauling in its reflection.
The sad flat light withdrew
as Yuko's tongue from a deep kiss.